POETICAL INSPIRATION IN OLD NORSE AND OLD ENGLISH POETRY

By

ANTHONY FAULKES

PROFESSOR OF OLD ICELANDIC
IN THE UNIVERSITY OF BIRMINGHAM

*The Dorothea Coke Memorial Lecture
in Northern Studies
delivered at University College London
28 November 1997*

PUBLISHED FOR THE COLLEGE BY THE
VIKING SOCIETY FOR NORTHERN RESEARCH
LONDON

© UNIVERSITY COLLEGE LONDON 1997
PRINTED IN THE UNIVERSITY OF BIRMINGHAM

ISBN: 0 903521 32 6

POETICAL INSPIRATION IN OLD NORSE AND OLD ENGLISH POETRY

IN THE VENERABLE BEDE'S ACCOUNT of the earliest known Anglo-Saxon poet Caedmon, we are told that Caedmon was an unlettered herdsman who was unable to take part in the evening entertainment of his fellows because he could not sing. One night after he had left a party early because of his embarrassment an angel came to him in a dream and told him to sing of creation, and the result is Caedmon's hymn, a short poem about God's creation of the world for men, the most remarkable thing about which is its complicated verbal and metrical structure. Thereafter Caedmon was found to have a gift for poetry; and it is interesting to note that his later poems were evidently produced by the learned monks of the monastery retelling to him stories from the Bible which he is said to have chewed over like a cow chewing the cud and to have reproduced in poetical language with great sweetness (*Hist. eccl.* IV 24).

From Bede's account it is clear that the divine gift Caedmon received was one of expression, the ability to tell existing stories in verse form, 'what oft was thought but ne'er so well express'd'. If he was inspired, it was not the content, but the language that he was inspired with, as is argued by C. L. Wrenn in 'The Poetry of Caedmon' (1946, 286), who suggests that the real miracle of Caedmon was that an unlettered peasant should become able to use the style and manner of learned court poetry. There is a close analogue to the story of Caedmon in the Old Icelandic story of Hallbjǫrn hali in *Flateyjarbók* (*ÍF* IX 227–9). His problem was that he wanted to compose an elegy for an earlier poet but could not find the words. He fell asleep on the poet's grave mound and the dead man came out to him in his dream and gave him the ability to compose poetry, instructing him to compose in as complex a metrical and verbal style as possible. One interesting similarity between the stories of Caedmon and Hallbjǫrn is that while both are said to have gone on to compose much other poetry, no further verse by either of them has been recorded.

Stories about individuals receiving inspiration in composing poetry from supernatural sources are widespread, but what I want to compare with Bede's account of Caedmon's inspiration is what Snorri Sturluson wrote about poetry in Iceland in the thirteenth century. Snorri is one of the few writers of medieval Scandinavia who express clear critical attitudes about the nature of vernacular poetry, and although he was writing towards the end of the period when oral skaldic poetry was cultivated in the North, it is likely that his views about poetry would have been shared by many poets and their audiences in his time and earlier. He has a myth about the origin of poetry in his Edda, according to which poetical inspiration is given to gods and men by Óðinn in the form of an alcoholic drink brewed from the blood of a person of immense wisdom created from the spittle produced by two races of gods to seal their truce after their war together. This drink had to be recovered by Óðinn after it had been in the possession first of dwarfs and then of giants, and when he escaped with it back to the other gods he carried it in his stomach while flying in the form of an eagle; he was chased by another eagle and could not prevent some of the liquid from being expelled backwards; that part of it was left for rhymesters or poetasters. The rest which he was able to bring up into containers in Ásgarðr was for the gods, and for human poets and scholars.

There are many analogues to this story too in the mythology of various countries, some of them well outside the area of Germanic culture. Skaldic poets frequently alluded to the story in their poetry. It seems at first sight that this would support the idea of poetry having being seen in medieval Scandinavia as an inspirational activity of which the symptoms were similar to drunkenness. Thus the seventeenth-century Icelandic poet Magnús Ólafsson in his essay on Norse poetry published in 1636 speaks of a poet reciting appearing to be *vino madens* and uses the term *skáldvingl* or *poetica vertigo*:

> Further, our poetry also has this peculiarity: whereas in ordinary languages anyone can put together poems in accordance with the

fashion of his country, force the words into some sort of rhythmical pattern, and by practice achieve some fluency; in ours no one becomes a poet, or can put together even the simplest kind of poem without great labour, however much he wants to, unless he is especially gifted with poetic inspiration. And this inspiration, like other natural passions, affects some more violently and others more gently. Some produce good poetry after long working out, others pour out all kinds of poems extempore with a more violent kind of impulse, so that whatever they try to express turns out to be poetry, as that most ingenious Roman poet once claimed of his own poetic fluency, and they find verse just as easy as prose. Further, this sort of quality reveals itself by clear signs straightway at a very early age. Nor must it be forgotten that this activity of the spirit is hottest at the time of the new moon, and you would say that an outstanding poet explaining poetical matters to others, or occupied in delivering poetry, was under the influence of drink, was afflicted with a rather severe attack of melancholy, or was seized by some madness; and often this quality can be detected even in strangers from a certain particular mannerism which we call *skáldvingl* or poetical delirium.

Magnús Ólafsson, however, was influenced by Renaissance attitudes to poetry (and the Roman poet he refers to is Ovid, *Tristia* IV x 25), though he may not actually have read Shakespeare's words about the poet's eye in a fine frenzy rolling or the lunatic, the lover and the poet, and I know of no medieval Icelandic stories of individual poets being inspired either literally or metaphorically to compose particular poems by draughts of the mead of poetry, and although Óðinn is sometimes referred to by poets (most notably by Egill Skalla-Grímsson) as the giver of the gift of poetic expression, he is never invoked by poets in Scandinavia in the way that the Muses were invoked by classical poets. What Óðinn's mead gives is not the inspiration to compose a poem, but the ability and skill to express oneself in verse (and the ability to be a scholar). Poets speak of composition and performance as pouring out Óðinn's mead, not as drinking it; *Skáldskaparmál* verses 4 and 17 by Skáld-Refr are ambiguous, but verse 18 by Einarr skálaglamm is clear. Refr said this:

(4) Often the kind man brought me to the raven-god's [Óðinn's] holy drink [instructed me in poetry].

(17) To you we owe Falr's cups [the mead of poetry], noble Slaughter-Gautr [Óðinn].

Einarr skálaglamm said this:

> (18) I shall succeed in bailing the draught of Host-Tyr's [Óðinn's] wine-vessel [the mead of poetry] before the ship-impeller [seaman, i. e. Earl Hákon]—I need no urging to that.

When skaldic poets refer to the receiving of Óðinn's mead, it is generally their hearers who do this, not the poets (*Skáldskaparmál* verses 27, 28, 29). The role of Óðinn is made more complex by references to the god Bragi as also being a patron of poetry, though there are no stories to illustrate in what way he relates to human poets. It may be added that there is not a close connection between poetry and religious ritual expressed in Old Norse poetry, except perhaps in some eddic verse.

Much—though not all—skaldic poetry is characterised by complexity of diction and metre. There are several anecdotes illustrating the difficulties of understanding it (as well as some indicating the difficulty of composing it; Snorri refers to this in *Háttatal* in the introduction to stanza 17), and some that indicate attitudes to its complexity. These anecdotes are mostly from the thirteenth century, and so do not necessarily tell us about attitudes to poetry in the Viking Age, but they are probably contemporary with Snorri and reinforce the impression gained from his writings. The puzzle element in Icelandic poetry is dominant; the same word, *ráða*, is used of interpreting poetry as of interpreting runes, riddles and dreams. Snorri in several places in *Skáldskaparmál* refers to poetry in terms of concealment. He makes Ægir describe a kenning for poetry as *vel fólgit í rúnum*, 'concealed well in runes'; Bragi had just referred to the use of this kenning as *vér felum í rúnum eða í skáldskap svá*, 'we conceal [it] in runes or in poetry thus' (the basic meaning of the word *rún* is 'secret'). Ægir refers to other kennings as *myrkt*, 'obscure' (*Edda Snorra Sturlusonar* 1931, 81–3). Snorri refers to the purpose of *Skáldskaparmál* as to help young poets *at kunna skilja þat er hulit er kveðit*, 'to be able to understand what is composed so as to be concealed' (*Edda Snorra Sturlusonar* 1931, 86). He also speaks ironically of the use in poetry of *gera ofljóst at vant er at skilja*, 'making too clear so that it is difficult to understand'. His account of *ofljóst* gives a good idea of how important he thought the puzzle element in poetry (*Edda Snorra Sturlusonar* 1931, 193):

Læti means two things. Noise is called *læti*, disposition *(œði)* is called *læti*, and *œði* also means fury. *Reiði* also has two meanings. It is called *reiði* [wrath] when a man is in a bad temper, the gear *(fargervi)* of a ship or horse is called *reiði*. *Far* also has two meanings. *Fár* is anger, *far* is a ship. People frequently use such vocabulary so as to compose with concealed meaning, and this is usually called word-play (*ofljóst* [obvious]). People call it *lið* [joint] on a person where the bones meet, *lið* is a word for ship, *lið* [troop] is a word for people. It is also called *lið* [help] when someone gives another assistance (*liðsinni*). *Líð* is a word for ale. There is what is called a *hlið* [gateway] in an enclosure, and *hlið* is what people call an ox, and *hlíð* is a slope. These distinctions can be made use of in poetry so as to create word-play which is difficult to understand, if it is a different distinction of meaning that has to be taken than the previous lines seemed before to indicate. Similarly there are also many other such words where the same term applies to several things.

Middle English poetry is claimed to have a large element of the desire for concealment in its purpose and style by A. C. Spearing (*Readings in Medieval Poetry* 1989, 97). In *Gísla saga* (ch. 18), the hero (who is a poet) is depicted as reciting a poem 'which he should have kept to himself'. It is overheard by his sister, who 'got the verse by heart from the one hearing, and goes home, and by then she has worked out its meaning.' In the verse Gísli has revealed his guilt for the secret killing of her husband (*ÍF* VI 58–9). There is a comparable riddling confession of guilt in *Grettis saga* verse 11 (ch. 16; *ÍF* VII 47). In *Sneglu-Halla þáttr* (*ÍF* IX 263–95), which is even more obviously fictional than *Gísla saga*, but which nevertheless must express attitudes and values of the thirteenth century, the hero is depicted as not only a poet but a joker; he comes to the court of Harold Godwineson and recites a poem supposedly in his honour. The king and his court are unable to understand the poem immediately, and when the poet asks for his reward the king orders silver to be poured over his head so that he can keep as a reward an amount comparable to what the audience retained of his poem. Halli smears tar over his hair so that a lot of the silver sticks, and then makes good his escape, because he knows that eventually the king will realise that the poem was nonsense. This is clearly a satire on the incomprehensibility of Viking poetry; the point does not seem to be the linguistic barrier between Icelanders and Englishmen in the eleventh century, since saga-writers do not seem to acknowledge that there was one. In *Gunnlaugs saga* it is claimed that then the same language was spoken in England as in Norway and Denmark (*ÍF* III 70).

Two verses supposed to have been spoken by Haraldr harðráði before the Battle of Stamford Bridge in 1066 have been taken to demonstrate that king's preference for elaborate and obscure verse. The story is told in Snorri Sturluson's *Heimskringla* (*ÍF* XXVIII, 187–8). He is said to have left his armour in his ship and is going to have to fight without it. He states this in a simple, straightforward and quite expressive verse in the simple metre of eddic poetry. Then he says, *Þetta er illa kveðit ok mun verða at gera aðra vísu betri*, 'that is badly composed and I shall now make another better verse', and utters a rather complex verse in very involved skaldic style which is really rather difficult to interpret, though there are plenty that are worse.

I now want to look at some examples of skaldic verse and the techniques used in them, and what Snorri says about them, to see what impression we can get about what was actually valued in this poetry when it was composed. Snorri discusses two aspects of poetry at length in his Edda, vocabulary and metre; he has very little to say about other aspects of it such as content. In his discussion of vocabulary he spends most time on nominal groups where instead of referring to a person or thing by its normal name, a poet replaces (or conceals) that name with another, which may be a poetical term like 'steed' for 'horse', or a kenning, which has at least two elements, such as when gold is called 'fire of the sea' or a king 'distributor of gold'. Many of these terms are not metaphorical and few can be described as images; generally they do not focus on the characteristics of individual persons or things, but convey the general concept of gold object or ruler and so on without expressing any feature of them either as individuals or as being in a particular situation. That is, a ruler will be a distributor of gold even when he is fighting a battle and gold will be called the fire of the sea even when it is in the form of a man's arm-ring on his arm. If the man wearing the gold ring is fighting a battle on land the mention of the sea will have no relevance to his situation at all and does not contribute to the picture of the action being described.

Among the practical difficulties of understanding and translating such verse is the problem of working out the syntactical relations of words and phrases and knowing how involved and complex they are supposed to be. In an inflected language like Icelandic, understanding the functions of words depends less on their position in the sentence than on their grammatical form, so that it is often possible in verse to depart from the normal word-order without making the functions of words ambiguous, and skaldic poets use this facility extensively, so that not only the order of elements in the sentence is varied, but words belonging together as parts of a single phrase are often separated or interwoven with parts of other phrases. In kennings, one element is generally in the genitive case, and in most words, though indeed not in all, the genitive is easily recognised and distinct from other forms of the word. But when there are two kennings juxtaposed, each of which contains a genitive, it can sometimes be difficult to see which genitive belongs with which base-word.

I am afraid I am now going to get rather technical, and I am sorry if this induces any feeling of poetical vertigo in you, but it is necessary to go into technicalities to understand the poetry, and this is believed to be oral poetry which was understood orally by its original audience. There is a difficulty in knowing how to present skaldic verse for a modern audience, though I am convinced that it is possible to make it meaningful even to those with little knowledge of Old Norse. It is common in modern editions of skaldic verses to present the text in 'prose word-order', i. e. to print the verse first in its manuscript form and then to re-arrange the words so that those that belong to the same phrase come together. Snorri himself uses this method of explication (i. e. re-ordering the words as prose) with two verses in *Háttatal* (which is a poem he himself composed), verses 17–18. This is mainly because in these verses he is illustrating *refhvǫrf*, where words of opposite meanings are juxtaposed though they do not always have those opposite meanings in the verse as a whole. His verse 17 and explanation (which is not entirely a re-ordering

of the words, but also in part a prose paraphrase) are as follows.
The prose word-ordering is printed in bold type.

> Síks glóðar verr sœkir
> slétt skarð hafi jarðar;
> hlífgranda rekr hendir
> heit kǫld loga ǫldu;
> fljótt válkat skilr fylkir
> friðlæ—rǫðul‹s› sævar
> ránsið ræsir stǫðvar—
> reiðr—glaðr frǫmum meiðum.

... Hér eru sýnd í þessi vísu sextán orðtǫk sundrgreinilig, ok eru flest ofljós til rétts mals at fœra, ok skal þá svá upp taka: **síks glóð**, þat er gull; **sœkir** gulls, þat er maðr; hann **verr skarð jarðar hafi slétt**, þat eru Firðir, svá heitir fylki i Nóregi; **hlífgrandi**, þat er vápn; **hendir loga ǫldu** er maðr, er **rekr kǫld heit** sverðinu, þat er at hegna ósiðu; **fljótt válkat** má þat kalla er skjótt ráðit er, þat **skilr** hann af ófriðinum; konungr heitir **fylkir, ránsið ræsir stǫðvar sævar rǫðuls frǫmum meiðum**.

... Here are demonstrated in this stanza sixteen phrases of contrary meanings, and most of them have to be turned to their proper meaning by means of word-play, and this is how it is to be understood: **ditchglede**, i. e. gold; **attacker** of gold, that is a man; he **defends the cleft of land smoothed by the sea**, i. e. Firðir, this is the name of a district in Norway; **with shield-harmer**, i. e. a weapon; **thrower of wave-flame** is a man, who **drives away cold threats** with the sword, that is to punish wickedness; **hastily-weighed** may be said of what is unpremeditated, he **perceives** this from the hostility; a king is called *fylkir* [leader]; **the ruler puts a stop to the plundering habits of bold sea-sun-trees**.

Verse 18 is similar. This sort of effect, where words have to be understood in two meanings at once, must have been very difficult to convey in the pre-literary period. It is doubtful, however, whether this method of re-ordering the words of a verse into 'prose' word-order could have been used in the pre-literary period (it is only with these two verses of *Háttatal*, and in a less exhaustive way, verses 4–6 of the same poem, that Snorri himself uses it), though a somewhat similar second explanatory text was apparently preserved orally alongside the 'real' text in the case of Vedic poems, which are probably much deeper in the oral period of their culture than any Scandinavian verse is in its (Macdonell 1917, xii–xiii). But it is difficult to see how people could have understood complex skaldic verse without some such assistance, and in particular how the audience could have been made to realise which words belonged together in a verse when there is a genuine possibility of taking them in two ways.

In my explanations I prefer not to re-order the words, since I think that the word-order not only embodies the structure of the verse, but also to a large extent the meaning, and I think it unlikely that this procedure would have been used in pre-literary times in Scandinavia. So I use the resources of the computer to identify which words belong together and how they can be represented in English; this method is in fact rather like that of E. A. Kock in his edition in *Den Norsk-Isländska Skaldediktningen* (1946–9). The asterisks mark words that have been unavoidably emended. Translation on its own cannot hope to reproduce much of the meaning or effect of the original. The numbers are the numbers of the verses in Finnur Jónsson's edition of *Edda Snorra Sturlusonar* of 1931.

An example of how words can be taken to belong to different phrases is found in this verse of Einarr Skúlason describing an ornamented axe:

(193) Blóðeisu liggr bæði
       bjargs tveim megin geima
       sjóðs—á ek søkkva stríði—
       snær ok eldr—at mæra.

> There lies on each side of the blood-ember's head (the head of the gold-adorned axe) both the purse's snow and ocean's fire; I must praise the punisher of Vikings.

There are two kennings for the decoration on the axe: *sjóðs snær* and *geima eldr*—or it might be *sjóðs eldr* and *geima snær*. Are they differentiated as gold and silver, or are they, contrary to our intuition, just general kennings for precious metal, as is implied by Snorri's commentary to verse 194 and the short anonymous treatise on kennings that Finnur Jónsson called 'Den lille Skálda' (*Edda Snorra Sturlusonar* 1931, 256/22: *gull má kenna til snæs ok íss*, 'gold can be referred to as snow and ice')? The kenning *søkkva stríði* is also ambiguous: *søkk* can mean 'gold', and *søkkva stríði* could mean 'destroyer, i. e. dispenser of gold, generous prince'.

My next example is anonymous:

(317) *Ǫrgildi var ek (Eldi‹s›)   [MS Ǫrgildis]
       áls Fjǫrgynjar (mála)
       dyggr; sé heiðr ok hreggi
       (hrynbeðs) ár steðja.

I was loyal to the liberal payer of Fjǫrgyn's eel's [serpent's] tinkling bed, and honour be to the storm of the river-anvil-[rock-]Eldir's [giant's] speech.

The two complicated kennings in this verse (referring to the same generous man) can be analysed in two quite different ways without the meaning being much affected, since the basewords (*ǫrgildi, hreggi;* both dative, with *ek var dyggr* and *sé ok heiðr*) are in the context synonymous ('liberal payer'; 'storm, destroyer') and both the strings of determinants mean 'gold': *ǫrgildi hrynbeðs Fjǫrgynjar áls* and *hreggi ár steðja Eldis mála*, or *ǫrgildi ár steðja Eldis mála* and *hreggi hrynbeðs Fjǫrgynjar áls*.

The next example is from Einarr skálaglamm's *Vellekla*:

(223)   Ne sigbjarka serkir
        sómmiðjungum rómu
        Hárs við Hǫgna skúrir
        hléðut fast of séðir.

The three nouns *serkir, (sóm)miðjungum, skúrir* are base-words in kennings for, respectively, mail-coats, warriors, missiles: *Ne hléðut fast of séðir serkir miðjungum við skúrir,* 'the firmly-sewn mail-coats did not defend warriors from missiles.' The words which may be determinants in these kennings are *sigbjarka, sóm-, rómu, Hárs, Hǫgna*. There seem to be too many of them, and it is difficult to see which base-word each belongs with. Presumably *Hǫgna* goes with *skúrir, sigbjarka* ('battle birches', i. e. warriors'': it is unusual to refer to men by feminine tree-names) with *serkir*, and *sómmiðjungum,* 'bow-giants' is another kenning for warriors. What do we do with *rómu Hárs*? Take it as a dative phrase, 'in Óðinn's tumult', i. e. 'in battle'? But *róma* means 'battle' on its own. Attaching *Hárs* or *rómu* to any of the other kennings results in redundant elements to the kennings, though it is not certain that such redundancy was avoided by skaldic poets; there is quite a lot of it in their work.

In many verses, two parallel statements are juxtaposed or interwoven; obviously if each has a nominative subject and/or accusative object, only the meaning of the verb can determine which subject and object go with which verb, as in this verse in an account of a battle by Óttarr svarti:

(340) Qrn drekkr undarn,   *Eagle drinks breakfast*
       ylgr fær at hræm sylg,   *she-wolf gets from corpses drink*
       opt rýðr úlfr køpt,   *often reddens wolf its jaws*
       ari getr verð þar.   *eagle gets food there.*

The question is, which of the two possible interpretations should we accept and prefer, and why, taking *undarn* as object of *drekkr* ('drinks breakfast') and *sylg* as object of *fær* ('gets drink') or vice versa ('drinks liquid, gets breakfast')? (There are not the same possibilities in lines 3 and 4.) The first, which is syntactically simpler, is preferred by E. A. Kock, the second, which is semantically more logical, by Finnur Jónsson. However they are taken, both phrases refer to the devouring of dead warriors by birds of prey, but *sylg* would fit better than *undarn* as the object of *drekkr*, giving interchange of the elements of the two clauses. Kock's interpretation makes the quatrain an example of Snorri's *áttmælt*, where each line is a separate integral statement. Trying to understand which interpretation the poet meant raises basic questions of the meaning of utterances of the kinds that the philosopher Wittgenstein puzzled over. What does it mean to say that when I say something I mean this rather than that when what I have said could mean either? His arguments would support the idea that skaldic verse too was a game, a social ritual, where the function of the activity was more important than the meaning or content of the utterances.

There is a similar kind of syntactical ambiguity in this verse about Þórr fighting a giant from Þjóðólfr of Hvinir's *Haustlǫng*:

(67) Þyrmðit Baldrs of barmi   *Baldr's brother spared not*
      —berg—sólgnum þar dólgi   *(rocks) the greedy enemy there*
      —hristusk, bjǫrg ok brustu,   *(shook, crags also shattered;*
      brann upphiminn—manna.   *the sky above burned) of men.*

The interwoven statement here can be taken as *berg hristusk, berg ok brustu,* or *hristusk bjǫrg ok berg brustu*. Both the verbs and both the nouns are near synonyms, and various orders are possible, though Kock prefers to take *berg* with *sólgnum* so that the parenthesis has only one subject. *Manna* could conceivably go with *upphiminn* rather than with *dólgi*. With these two suggestions adopted, lines 3 and 4 become integral statements and there is no parenthesis at all. It is doubtful whether that is what a medieval audience would have preferred, and 'sky of men' is a less normal expression than 'enemy of men' (= giant). Are normal expressions what we should expect in skaldic verse? Is logic a valid criterion of meaning and authorial intention? What are the underlying aesthetic preferences, for naturalness and simplicity or for complexity and puzzlement? There are also multiple possibilities of arranging the kennings in lines 5–8 of this stanza.

There is another example in the description of the death of the giant Þjazi in *Haustlǫng*:

(104) Hófu skjótt en skófu   *Began quickly and shaved*
skǫpt ginnregin brinna   *shafts mighty powers to burn*

Here there are two plural verbs, *skófu* and *hófu brinna*, and two plural nouns, *skǫpt* and *ginnregin*, which could each be either nominative or accusative. The two statements can be read 'shafts quickly began to burn, and the mighty powers shaved them', or 'they quickly began to burn and the mighty powers shaved shafts', or *skǫpt* could be read both as the subject of the one verb and as the object of the other, 'shafts quickly began to burn, and the mighty powers shaved shafts'. *Skjótt* could also, of course be taken with either clause or with both (the phenomenon of one word belonging to two separate clauses is discussed below, p. 18).

If there is more than one adverbial phrase in a verse containing more than one clause, it can be difficult to see which phrase goes in which clause. For instance, Bragi the Old describes Þórr's fishing for the Midgard serpent like this:

(42)   Vaðr lá Viðris arfa
             vilgi slakr er rakðisk,
             á Eynæfis ǫndri,
             Jǫrmungandr at sandi.

In this verse there are two clauses, the main clause *Vaðr Viðris arfa lá vilgi slakr*, 'Viðrir's son's (i. e. Þórr's) fishing-line lay by no means slack' and the subordinate clause *er rakðisk Jǫrmungandr*, 'when Jǫrmungandr (the Midgard serpent) uncoiled'. The two adverbial phrases *á Eynæfis ǫndri*, 'in Eynæfir's ski (on the boat)' and *at sandi*, 'on the sand' can each be taken with either verb, though as we picture the scene of Þórr's fishing for the Midgard serpent the first seems to go better with *lá* and the second with *rakðisk*.

(2)   *Now [there] is for steed-logs of the sea* [i. e. for sea-warriors]
       Nú er jódraugum ægis

      eagle's flight—and rings,   [i. e. birds of prey are gathering,
      arnar flaug—ok bauga,   a battle is taking place]

      I think that invitation they will receive
      hygg ek at heimboð þiggi

      of god of the hanged—over the field.   [i. e. of Óðinn in
      Hangagoðs—of vangi.   Valhalla]

In this verse attributed to Hávarðr halti the 'prose word-order' is obtained by exchanging the last two words in the first couplet with the last two in the second. This is required not by the syntax, for it is grammatically possible to read the words in the original order, but by the sense, for *bauga* will not do as a parallel to either *arnar* or *flaug*, and the adverbial phrase *of vangi* will not do with *þiggi heimboð Hangagoðs*. The battle is taking place on the field, and the warriors will receive Óðinn's hospitality and plunder. And although the order is required by the verse-form (to provide the hendings), it is difficult to believe that it is that that has determined the order, for there are plenty of alternative words that could have been used to express the meaning. The poet must have wanted the 'unnatural' word-order.

Eysteinn Valdason describes Þórr's fight with the Midgard sepent as follows:

(47)   *So it happened/reacted* **planks**
           Svá brá viðr at **sýjur**

           COALFISH *made run forward* **broad**
           SEIÐR rendi fram **breiðar**

EARTH'S; *out on the gunwale*
JARÐAR; út at borði

Ullr's stepfather's (Þórr's) fists banged
Ulls mág[s] hnefar skullu.

It is the syntax rather than the kenning that is obscure in this verse. *Brá við* could be impersonal, 'it happened', or *seiðr jarðar* ('earth's coalfish', i. e. the Midgard serpent) could be the subject, 'the serpent reacted'; *rendi* is causative 'to make run' and usually takes a dative object, but can also take an accusative object (then generally with the object being a liquid, to pour), or be intransitive. 'So it happened that the earth's coalfish made the broad planks run forward' or 'so the earth's coalfish reacted that the broad planks ran forward'. The meaning of the two interpretations is not very different, and there seems no way to decide between them. While there is little support for the use of *rendi* with an accusative object, if *sýjur* is the subject the verb needs to be emended to *rendu*. Finnur Jónsson achieves further complexity by taking the last line and a half as the *at*-clause, and *breiðar sýjur rendu fram* as the second main clause: 'the earth's coalfish reacted so that out on the gunwale Ullr's stepfather's (Þórr's) fists banged; the broad planks ran forward.' This is the sort of interweaving of clauses that Kock condemns as an unnatural and over-academic interpretation, though it certainly can be argued that the natural *meaning* of the verse is that the serpent's reaction caused Þórr's fists to bang on the gunwale, rather than that it was the cause of the boat moving forward; but Finnur's version does involve assuming a most unnatural word-order.

Arnórr jarlaskáld in *Þorfinnsdrápa* says:

(297) Bitu sverð—en þar *þurðu— [MS þurðir]
       þunngjǫr fyrir Mǫn sunnan
       Rǫgnvalds kind—und randir
       ramlig fólk—ins gamla.

The most obvious interpretation of this would be to take *Rǫgnvalds ins gamla kind*, 'Rǫgnvaldr the Old's descendant' = Earl Þorfinnr as the object of *þunngjǫrð sverð bitu*, 'thinly made swords pierced', but from the context of the verse we know that it is not about Earl Þorfinnr being wounded, but about his victory. *Bitu* must therefore be without an object and *kind* must be dative of advantage. 'Thinly made swords pierced for Rǫgnvaldr the Old's descendant; and mighty armies pressed forward under their shields there.' Would the possibility of a misunderstanding have been understood as a joke? *Fyrir Mǫn sunnan*, 'to the south of the Isle of Man' could go with either clause or both, and should perhaps be understood with *þar*.

As well as the separation of words belonging to the same phrase, there are clear examples of the parts of a compound word being separated from each other (the classical term for this is tmesis), and even of the separation of the parts of two compound words within the same half-verse. If the separated first elements are placed before other words than those they belong with, it can be difficult to be sure which words they are part of, and there are examples of elements of a pair of compound words being interchanged.

One of the clearest and most undeniable examples of tmesis is:

(101/3–4) Þá var Ið- með jǫtnum   *Then was Ið- among the giants*
-uðr nýkomin sunnan.   *-uðr newly come from the south.*

Iðuðr is a form of the name of *Iðunn*, the keeper of the gods' apples of eternal youth, who was abducted by the giant Þjazi. The two parts of her name, although they exist as separate words, make no sense separately in this sentence.

Another is:

(93/4)   ó- fyr -skǫmmu   *not ago a short [time], i. e. long ago.*

Ó- corresponds to the English prefix *un-*, and like it is not normally separated from the word it negates. Both these examples are from *Haustlǫng*, and it is interesting that some of the most confusing of these syntactical complexities are found in poetry on mythological topics, though I cannot see that there can be any religious reason for the poet to be obscure in these particular verses. If there is a connection the poet might be considered more likely to be parodying priestly language than just using it.

Not all kennings consist of base words with genitives; some consist of compound words where the first half of the compound replaces a genitive. Tmesis dividing such compounds is even more difficult to understand when the elements of a word are not only separated by more than a line, but are in reverse order. This example is from Eilífr Guðrúnarson's *Þórsdrápa*:

(78)   *There into the forest against the forest's*
Þar í **mǫrk** fyrir **markar**

noisily chattering wind [= current] they set
málhvettan byr settu

(the slippery wheel-knobs [stones] did not)
(ne hvélvǫlur hálar)

fishing-net shooting adders [spears] (sleep)
háf- skotnaðra (sváfu).

There they pushed shooting-snakes [spears] in the fishing-net-forest [river] against the talkative [noisy] fishing-net-forest wind [current]. The slippery wheel-knobs [stones] did not lie asleep.

Here, *háf-* is taken as the first element in the compound *háfmǫrk* and at the same time as the first element in the compound *háfmarkar* (in both cases making a kenning for river, 'fishing-net-forest'). Words that are to be taken as part of two separate phrases or clauses in Old English poetry are discussed by Bruce Mitchell in *An Invitation to Old English* 1995, 70. Bruce Mitchell spoils his argument for the existence of such constructions by accusing those who do not accept them of being insensitive, which is like accusing those who cannot see fairies of being blind; but according to Roberta Frank in *Old Norse Court Poetry* 1978, 112, a similar feature occurs in Japanese poetry. There is a further possible example in *Skáldskaparmál* in verse 104, quoted above.

In this verse from Úlfr Uggason's *Húsdrápa* the parts of the kenning-compound are again separated by two lines:

(64)   ***Helpful in counsel** acts gods'*
Ráðgegninn bregðr **ragna**

strip of land at Singasteinn
rein- at Singasteini

renowned against mighty sly
frægr við firna *slœgjan   [MS slœgjum]

*Fárbauti's son **defender***
Fárbauta *mǫg **-vári**.   [MS mǫgr]

Here *rein* goes with *vári* to make a compound: *frægr ráðgegninn ragna reinvári*, 'the renowned helpful in counsel defender of the god's strip of land', i. e. Heimdallr, defender of Bifrǫst. Tmesis can be avoided, as Kock points out, by replacing *rein* with the genitive *reinar* (*Notationes norrænæ* § 1952), though this makes the metre less normal.

(260)   Fjarðlinna óð fannir
        fast vetrliði rastar;
        hljóp of *húna -gnípur
        hvals *rann- íugtanni.

The winter-survivor [bear] of the current [i. e. the ship] waded fast the drifts of fjord-serpents [waves]; the greedy-tooth [bear] of the mast-head [i. e. the ship] ran over the whale's house-tops.

This is attributed to Markús Skeggjason and describes a sea-voyage. The kennings in the second couplet are *húna [MS hvíta] íugtanni* and *hvals ranngnípur*. Emending *rann* [MS *þann*] to *ranns* would get rid of the tmesis, but the two kennings remain with their determinants effectively exchanged. Cf. Frank 1978, 46–7. Another striking example of double tmesis is found in another verse of *Þórsdrápa:*

(90)   . . . salvanið- -Synjar
        sigr hlaut arin- *-bauti.   [MS arinbrauti]

The subject of *sigr hlaut*, 'gained victory' is a kenning for Þórr, *arin-Synjar salvaniðbauti*, 'beater of the frequenter of hearth-stone-Syn's dwelling', though Kock (*Notationes norrænæ* § 467) makes it into one for giantesses, acc. with the preposition *of*. Here again the tmesis (but not the exchange of determinants) could be avoided by making both *salvanið* and *arin* genitive.

There is an instructive example of how the possibility of seeing maximum complexity in a verse was dealt with in the thirteenth century in Snorri's commentary to the next verse, which is attributed to Víga-Glúmr; this commentary at the same time demonstrates Snorri's acknowledgement that the elements of compound kennings can be interchanged:

(255) Rudda ek sem jarlar   *I fought my way like earls*
      —orð *lék á því—forðum   *I had a reputation for this formerly*
      með veðrstǫfum Viðris   *with weather-staves of Viðrir's*
      vandar mér til *landa.   *wand to win lands.*

The MS has *lér* in line 2 and *handa* in line 4. It is difficult to know which clause *forðum*, 'formerly' goes with, but more significant is that Snorri's commentary analyses the kenning for warriors as *stafir vandar Viðris veðrs*, 'staves of the wand of Viðrir's weather' instead of the more obvious *stafir veðrs Viðris vandar*, 'staves of the weather of Viðrir's wand'. Viðrir is a name for Óðinn, whose weather is battle and whose wand is the sword. Snorri's interpretation involves exchanging *veðr* and *vandar*. Such interchanging of the elements of a complex kenning is certainly found, however, as in the next verse, which is attributed to Egill Skalla-Grímsson, who seems not to have been averse to word-play. This is one of the best-known examples of tmesis:

(140) Upp skulum órum sverðum,   *Aloft shall we make our swords*
     úlfs tannlituðr, glitra;   *O stainer of wolves' teeth, shine;*
     eigum dáð at drýgja   *we have daring deeds to do*
     í dalmiskunn fiska.   *in the valley-mercy of fish.*

The stainer of wolves' teeth is the warrior addressed in the verse, who gives wolves blood to drink from his dead enemies. The last line has to be read *í miskunn dalfiska*, 'in the mercy of valley-fish'; valley-fish are snakes, their mercy or grace is the summer when they come out of hibernation, and this can either be interpreted as tmesis (*dal-* separated from *-fiska*) or as transference of one of the elements of a kenning from a determinant to the base-word. This does give a more regular rhythm to the line, but can hardly be said to be determined by metrical considerations.

An example of a particularly complex verse is this one, which is another quatrain from Einarr skálaglamm's *Vellekla*:

(34)   *Rushes wave before prince*
      Eisar *vágr fyrir vísa,   [MS vargr]

      works of Óðinn profit me
      verk Rǫgnis mér *hagna,   [MS hǫgna]

      pounds mead-container's swell
      þýtr Óðreris alda

      always sea's against skerry of songs   [i. e. teeth]
      aldr hafs við fles galdra.

There seem to be three kennings for poetry here, each of which is the subject of a sentence. *Vágr* (wave), *verk* (works), *alda* (wave) look like base-words, the first and last in reference to the mead of poetry. *Rǫgnis* (Óðinn's), *Óðreris* (the mead-container's) and *hafs* (the sea's) look like determinants. Some commentators have by emendation produced alternatives to some of these, but they do not reduce the problems, which arise from the fact that the genitives do not seem to be closest to the nominatives they go with. *Verk Rǫgnis* (Óðinn's work) would make a recognisable kenning for poetry, and so would *Óðreris alda* (wave of the mead-container), but that leaves *vágr hafs* (or *aldrhafs*), 'wave of the ancient (?) sea' which would not. Unless one is prepared to guess at some radical emendation, it is difficult to avoid the conclusion that *fyrir* governs not *vísa* but *mér*, and the kennings are *vágr Rǫgnis* (Óðinn's wave), *verk vísa* (prince's work) and *alda hafs Óðreris* (wave of the sea of the mead-container).

It is interesting that such complexity so frequently occurs in verses that are actually about poetry and composition, and that the actual content of this ingenious verse amounts to little more than 'I am performing rewarding poetry before the prince'. It is a performative utterance rather than an informative one. It is the ritual that is important.

Word-play of various kinds is used by skaldic poets. There is an example of word-play using redundancy or deliberate tautology in a kenning in a verse of Einarr Skúlason:

(335) Hugins fermu bregðr harmi   *The troubler of Huginn's food*
     harmr.   *ends his trouble.*

The troubler of Huginn's food (carrion) is the one who eats it, i. e. Huginn himself, the raven; the trouble that he ends by eating it is his hunger.

One device that Snorri mentions several times is called *ofljóst*, literally (and ironically) 'too clear'. *Ofljóst* is a kind of word-play particularly used for personal names, where the name, or an element of it, is replaced by a synonym of the word as a common noun, e. g. Foglhildr for Svanhildr. Eilífr Guðrúnarson uses this device in a form reminiscent of crossword-puzzle clues for the name Hákon:

(36)   *You will have to, since of words*
     *Verði *þér, alls orða   [MS verðr ei]

for us grows about noble kinsman (Earl Hákon)
oss grœr of kon *mæran   [MS mærar]
on mind-land of mead-container   [breast, heart,
á sefreinu Sónar   where poetry is stored]
seed, decide upon friendly gifts
sáð, vingjǫfum ráða.

There are two kennings in this verse, *orða sáð* (seed of words = poetry) and *sefreinu Sónar* (the poet's breast), though some people prefer to take them as *sáð Sónar* (seed of the mead-container) and *sefreinu orða* (sedge-land of words = breast or tongue). In addition *kon mæran* seems to mean Hákon (*há-* = high, noble, *mærr* = famous, glorious, noble; *kon* = kinsman, son, as well as being an element in the name Hákon). This kind of *ofljóst* is where a word is effectively replaced by a synonym of a homonym. The same name is split into two parts by tmesis in a verse attributed to Queen Gunnhildr in *Fagrskinna* (*ÍF* XXIX 75).

The name of Óðinn's consort Jǫrð (whose name means earth) is frequently replaced by a kenning and instead of talking about land or country, Óðinn's wife can be referred to, for example in this verse from Hallfreðr's *Hákonardrápa* about Earl Hákon winning land:

(10)   Sannyrðum spenr sverða
             *snarr þiggjandi viggjar   [MS þvarr]
             *barrhaddaða byrjar   [MS bjarr haddaða]
             *biðkván *und sik Þriðja.   [MS bifkván of]

The keen wind-steed-[ship-]taker [sea-farer, Earl Hákon] lures under himself [wins] with the true language of swords [battle] the pine-haired deserted wife of Third [Óðinn; his deserted wife is Jǫrð, earth, i. e. the land of Norway].

The latent sexual imagery here and in other poems on the same theme is likely to have been particularly relished by the earl's followers; it is unlikely to have any connection with myths about the ruler wedding his realm. The gaining of the earl's land is described as rape, not marriage. The number of emendations required in this and other verses in Snorri's Edda implies that scribes did not find them easy to understand.

Refhvarf is given particular attention in Snorri's *Háttatal*, though it is not common in earlier poets, and some examples of his use of this device were mentioned earlier. This is where two words are juxtaposed which have antithetical meanings, though in many of his examples the words are used with other meanings that are not antithetical, e. g. in verse 20:

> Hélir hlýr at stáli,
> hafit fellr, en svífr þelli
> (ferð dvol firrisk) harða
> fram mót lagar glammi.
> Vindr réttr váðir bendir;
> vefr rekr á haf snekkjur;
> veðr þyrr; vísa iðjur
> (varar fýsir skip) lýsa.

> The bow [/warms] freezes at the prow, the sea [/lifted] falls but the timber glides hard forwards against [/back] the water's uproar; the crew [/movement] is deprived of rest. The direct [/straightens] wind [/twists] bends the sails; the cloth [/folds] drives [/unfolds] the warships over the sea; the weather [/paces] whistles [rushes]; the ship is eager for [/exhorts] harbour [/warns]; the labours reflect glory on the ruler.

Thus in this kind of verse words have to be understood in one sense in order for the reader or listener to understand the meaning, but in another in order to appreciate the effect of the antithesis. It is a series of puns.

Substitution of a word by one that is a near synonym occurs in *nýgervingar*. Snorri's example is in kennings for gold of the type 'fire of the sea', which according to ch. 33 of *Skáldskaparmál* originated with the story of how Ægir, whose name means 'sea', used shining gold to illuminate his hall:

> So this is the story of the origin of gold being called fire or light or brightness of Ægir, Rán or Ægir's daughters, and from such kennings the practice has now developed of calling gold fire of the sea and of all terms for it, since Ægir and Rán's names are also terms for sea, and hence gold is now called fire of lakes or rivers and of all river-names.

It is in fact now difficult to know whether the kenning type 'fire of the water' = gold was originally used with reference to the sea or to a river or, as Snorri maintains, with reference to Ægir.

Elsewhere Snorri uses the term *nýgervingar* to mean extended metaphor, and this is effectively used by many poets. His complicated exemplification in *Háttatal* verse 6 gives rise to another of his detailed interpretations:

> Sviðr lætr sóknar naðra
> slíðrbraut jǫfurr skríða;
> ótt ferr rógs ór réttum
> ramsnákr fetilhamsi;
> linnr kná sverða sennu
> sveita bekks at leita;
> ormr þyrr vals *at varmri   [MS ór]
> víggjǫll sefa stígu.

The wise prince makes the adders of battle [swords] creep the scabbard-path [be drawn].
 The mighty war-snake goes swiftly from the straight strap-slough [scabbard].
 The sword-quarrel serpent can seek the stream of blood.
 The worm of the slain rushes along the mind's paths [men's breasts] to the warm war-river [flowing blood].

This is extended metaphor to call a sword a worm and use an appropriate determinant, and call the scabbard its paths and the straps and fittings its slough. It is in accordance with a worm's nature that it glides out of its slough and then often glides to water. Here the metaphor is so constructed that the worm goes to find the stream of blood where it glides along the paths of thought, i. e. men's breasts. Metaphor is held to be well composed if the idea that is taken up is maintained throughout the stanza. But if a sword is called a worm, and then a fish or a wand or varied in some other way, this is called a monstrosity (*nykrat*) and it is considered a defect.

Nykrat (literally 'made monstrous') is thus a kind of mixed metaphor. The effect of this is very similar to that of *refhvarf*, in that it involves conceptual contradictions. Though Snorri condemns it as unnatural (*ok þykkir þat spilla*, 'and it is thought to be a blemish', *Háttatal* 6/16) and his nephew Óláfr hvítaskáld in the Third Grammatical Treatise 80 calls it a *lǫstr*, 'fault', a type of *cacemphaton*, 'improper expression', many skaldic poets make effective use of the device (cf. Frank 1978, 52). Egill Skalla-Grímsson in one verse of his *Hǫfuðlausn* refers to a sword as saddle of the whetstone, sun of battle, digger of wounds, blood strip, sword-strap-ice. In a *lausavísa* which is one of the best descriptions of a sea-voyage in all skaldic verse, he calls the ship stem-bull and a sea-king's swan and the storm the giant of the mast and the wolf of the willow (*ÍF* II 172; Turville-Petre 1976, 23):

> The opposing (literally 'rowing in the opposite direction') mast-giant heavily strikes out a file with the chisel of storms before the prow out on the level stem-bull's path, and the cold-bringing willow-wolf grinds with it mercilessly in gusts Gestill's swan round the stem in front of the prow.

The example in the Fourth Grammatical Treatise 131 is a verse from *Jómsvíkinga saga* in which a cudgel is referred to by four different kennings, though they do not actually conflict. There are other good examples in Einarr skálaglamm's *Vellekla* (*Skáldskaparmál* verses 18, 27–8; see Foote and Wilson 1970, 365–6) and Þjóðólfr's *Haustlǫng* (*Skáldskaparmál* verse 92; see Marold 1983, 191; 1993, 291–7; Frank 1978, 46–8, 157–8).

In this lecture I have tried to give an impression of the various kinds of complexity that are to be found in skaldic verse, and of how difficult this makes the verses to understand. It seems that this complexity was one of the most highly valued aspects of skaldic art. If we were not sure for other reasons that most skaldic verse was composed and received orally in preliterary times, the style and manner of the verse would suggest that it was literary and meant to be read, as it clearly was by the time Snorri's Edda came to be written, as his treatment and discussion of it shows. Snorri was a very literary poet and scholar. If skaldic poetry was really composed and performed orally before that time, Viking poets were able to call upon a very high order of verbal ingenuity and skill indeed. Of course it is often argued that in an oral society, such skill, and the power of verbal memory that goes with it, was more developed anyway than it is in literate societies, and there may be something in this. There are nowadays people who can play chess without a chessboard and probably people who can solve crossword puzzles without using pen and paper. Composition and comprehension of a skaldic verse without having it on the page in front of one is not a more difficult achievement than these. But the picture this gives of the Viking is of a really rather intellectual type, far from the wild inspired figure evoked by Carlyle (in his work *On Heroes*), and I do not of course want to suggest that Vikings were incapable of high intellectual activity. Actually I think that the Viking was really rather an intellectual chap and thought of things that would astonish you. And Viking poets were probably more skilled in verbal expression, in spite of being less well educated in a formal sense, than Anglo-Saxon poets, and even than early Welsh and Irish poets, perhaps even than Provençal poets, while being less idiosyncratic and crazy than the writers of *Hisperica famina*.

Consider these examples of complex interweaving of sentences. The first is from Halldórr skvaldri's *Útfarardrápa*:

(379)   *You were able there their*
        Ér knáttuð þar þeira

        (you were never [shield's
        —þú vart aldrigi (skjaldar

        fire thundered though homes] of victory
        *leygr þaut of sjǫt) sigri

        bereft) treasure to divide.
        sviptr—gørsimum skipta.

The pattern here is abcba, with nesting of three statements each of 5–6 words. Shield's fire is a kenning for sword. (This verse is lacking in the Codex Regius; the Utrecht MS has *laugr* in line 3.)

From Kormakr's *Sigurðardrápa*:

(292)   Heyri sonr á **Sýrar**
        sannreynis **fentanna**
        ǪRR **greppa** *lætk uppi   [MS lætr]
        jast-Rín Haralds **mína**.

> Let the son of Haraldr's true trier [friend] listen; I cause to be heard my yeast-Rhine of the men of the Sýr of fen-teeth.

The kenning for the poem (the teeth of the fen are rocks, the Sýr of rocks is a giantess, whose men are giants; their yeast-liquid is the mead of poetry) is a complex one made more complex by the interweaving of its elements with the rest of the sentence. *Ǫrr*, 'generous', being nominative, could go with *sonr* or with *ek*; Kock prefers to make it the first half of the compound *ǫrgreppa*. If the first possibility is adopted, the syntactical pattern becomes abababab.

Another example from *Haustlǫng*:

(66) *Did all, but (of Ullr)*
 Knáttu ǫll, EN **Ullar**
 from end to end (because of the stepfather)
 ENDILÁG **fyrir mági**
 ground was battered by hail
 GRUND VAR GRÁPI HRUNDIN,
 the hawk's sanctuaries [the skies] burn
 *ginnunga vé *brinna [MS ginnjunga vé hrinna]

The word *en* seems to link the two clauses, though *Ullar fyrir mági*, 'because of Þórr') seems most likely to belong to the first ('all the hawk's sanctuaries did burn'), leaving *en* isolated. *Endilág* most naturally goes with *grund*, giving a pattern of elements abababa. Here too it might be possible to think of *Ullar fyrir mági* as belonging with both clauses or with the whole statement, rather than choosing between them.

The twelfth-century Icelandic poet Einarr Skúlason seems to have particularly liked certain kinds of complexity in his verse, and in these two examples he is describing an ornate weapon; the ornateness of the article described seems to be mirrored—though not actually described—in the ornateness of the verse:

(147) *Hǫrn's glorious child can I* [Hǫrn = Freyja; her child is
 Hróðrbarni kná ek Hǫrnar Hnoss = treasure, the precious axe]
 (we got a valuable treasure) possess,
 —hlutum dýran grip—stýra,
 ocean's fire rests on damager [ocean's fire = gold;
 brandr þrymr gjálfr‹s› á grandi damager of shield = axe]
 gold-wrapped of shield;
 gullvífiðu *hlífar; [MS hlíðar]
 seed (bears her mother's)
 -sáðs—berr sinnar móður—
 BATTLE-SWAN'S *granted me* [battle-swan's feeder = the ruler,
 SVANS unni mér GUNNAR who feeds ravens by fighting battles]
 FEEDER *of* **Fróði's** *servants* [seed of Fróði's servants is the
 fóstr- GŒÐANDI **Fróða**— gold ground by Fenja and Menja]

(Freyr's niece eyelashes' rain). [Freyr's niece = Hnoss, the
Freys nipt brá driptir. precious axe; her mother's eyelashes'
rain is the golden tears shed by Freyja,
i. e. the gold adornment on the axe]

Gullvífiðu in line 4 could go with *hróðrbarni* (it would fit semantically with this word; it is babies you wrap up rather than axes) or *grandi*. In line 5 *-sáðs* is supposed to be the second element of the compound *fóstrsáðs*, though Kock seeks to simplify the structure by reading *fóstrgœðandi* as one word and taking the kenning for gold as *Fróða sáðs*. This verse seems to me to be one that is virtually impossible to understand without writing it down and re-ordering the words. Freyja's daughter Hnoss is twice referred to without being named in this verse; in each case what is meant is *hnoss* as a common noun, meaning a treasure, referring to the axe. This is what is described above as *ofljóst*.

Snorri himself uses constructions of great complexity in *Háttatal* 98:

> Veit ek verðari
> þá er vell gefa,
> brǫndum beita
> ok búa snekkjur
> hæra hróðrar
> en heimdrega—
> unga jǫfra—
> en auðspǫruð.

I know of young princes that brandish swords and set up warships who are worthier of higher praise than a stay-at-home, ones who give gold than one sparing of wealth.

Here line 6 is parallel to lines 3–4 and line 8 to line 2. The 'prose word-order' would probably read the lines in the order 1, 7, 2, 8; 3, 4, 5, 6. (Finnur Jónsson in *Skjaldedigtning* B II 87 takes them in the order 1a, 7, 2a, 3, 4, 1b, 5, 6, 2b, 8.)

A device which seems very literary, and may be derived from some foreign model, is that of *vers rapportés*. This verse is attributed to Þórðr Særeksson, and Snorri quotes it simply to illustrate the kenning for Njǫrðr in line 6; he makes no comment on its form:

(59) Varð sjálf sonar— *Became herself of her son—*
nama snotr una— *Did not come to love—*
Kjalarr of tamði— *Kjallarr (Óðinn) tamed—*
kváðut Hamði— *It is said that Hamðir did not—*
—Goðrún bani —*Guðrún the slayer*
—goðbrúðr Vani —*the bride of the gods the Vanr*
—heldr vel mara —*rather well horses*
—hǫrleik spara. —*bow-warfare hold back.*

Here it is the meaning of the words and our knowledge of the stories referred to, rather than the grammar, that requires us to take the four statements as consisting of lines 1+5, 2+6, 3+7 and 4+8. The pattern is thus abcdabcd.

Finnur Jónsson in his great comprehensive edition of skaldic verse offered interpretations that frequently choose the most complicated ways of interpreting it even when simpler analyses are easy to see. E. A. Kock compiled a huge set of notes (*Notationes norrœnæ*) on the interpretations of skaldic verses, in which he frequently took issue with Finnur Jónsson for not choosing simpler solutions, accusing his interpretations of being 'desk interpretations' rather than ones that would be natural to oral poets, and a rather ill-tempered dispute then took place between the two scholars. Many of Kock's interpretations, however, in spite of being syntactically simpler, actually involve doing much more violence to the natural meanings of words and to natural grammar than is involved in Finnur's tortuous word-order, though neither he nor anyone else has been able to deduce any grammatical or metrical rules to explain the apparently arbitrary structure of interwoven sentences in skaldic verse. Neither Hans Kuhn's 'Sentence Particle Law' nor his theory about the caesura (1983, 89–97, 188–206) help very much, though they go some way towards it. And Finnur seems to me to have more feeling and intuition for the Old Norse language than Kock. From an examination of the complex and unnatural effects that are undoubtedly sometimes really used by Viking poets, and from Snorri's comments on them, it looks as though these poets did prefer complex meanings and effects to simple natural speech.

Nevertheless, I am doubtful about whether Viking poets ever intended verses to have more than one interpretation (as for instance in verse 193 quoted earlier), and whether that kind of ambiguity was part of the acknowledged skill in the activity; *ofljóst* uses words with double meanings, and the meaning is often concealed, or turns out to be other than at first seemed implied, but the verse as a whole only ever means one thing. There could always, of course, have been disagreements in the audience about how a particular verse ought to be read, but it seems that both poets and audiences wanted complexity.

Snorri speaks of the need for kennings to be in accordance with nature (*Skáldskaparmál* ch. 33: 'This is all considered acceptable when it is in accordance with genuine similarity and the nature of things [*með líkindum ok eðli*]'). But skaldic verse is in its essence unnatural, in diction, word-order, and grammar, and in ch. 33 Snorri is talking about word-substitution, not metaphor or images. The parallel with Viking art, particularly the interlace ornament that was popular throughout the Viking Age, has often been made. The Vikings' visual art, like their verbal art, contains representations of objects in the real world, but stylised and made complex to such an extent that it becomes very difficult to interpret, and the real nature of what is depicted seems to be deliberately concealed rather than revealed by the art. The reason for this, as with the use of runes, seems to be related not to the desire to be esoteric and hieroglyphic for religious or social or any other reasons, but to an aesthetic preference for complexity and puzzlement. Skaldic poetry seems to have been a restricted code to an even less extent than Anglo-Saxon or Old French poetry, which was probably confined to the aristocratic or religious ranks in society, whereas poetry seems to have been an almost universal activity among the Vikings, both as composers and audiences.

I have already mentioned Carlyle's notorious but unfortunately influential lectures *On heroes, hero-worship, and the heroic in history* (1841). He valued Old Norse poetry for its visionary qualities, and describes Óðinn as the originator of Old Norse poetry in this way in his first lecture:

> Strong sons of Nature; and here was not only a wild Captain and Fighter; discerning with his wild flashing eyes what to do, with his wild lion-heart daring and doing it; but a Poet too, all that we mean

> by a Poet, Prophet, great devout Thinker and Inventor,—as the truly Great Man ever is. A Hero is a Hero at all points; in the soul and thought of him first of all. This Odin, in his rude semi-articulate way, had a word to speak. A great heart laid open to take in this great Universe, and man's Life here, and utter a great word about it. A Hero, as I say, in his own rude manner; a wise, gifted, noble-hearted man. And now, if we still admire such a man beyond all others, what must these wild Norse souls, first awakened into thinking, have made of him! To them, as yet without names for it, he was noble and noblest; Hero, Prophet, God; *Wuotan*, the greatest of all. Thought is Thought, however it speak or spell itself. Intrinsically, I conjecture, this Odin must have been of the same sort of stuff as the greatest kind of men. A great thought in the wild deep heart of him! The rough words he articulated, are they not the rudimental roots of those English words we still use? He worked so, in that obscure element. But he was as a *light* kindled in it; a light of Intellect, rude Nobleness of heart, the only kind of lights we have yet; a Hero, as I say: and he had to shine there, and make his obscure element a little lighter,—as is still the task of us all.

That is, he regarded the obscurity of Old Norse verse as a result of its primitiveness. I regard the Vikings' techniques of verse composition as inspired, not what they say; and their obscurity as arising from sophisticated rhetorical complexity. If I wanted to find something to set against the Viking's reputation as raider, rapist and pillager to demonstrate how civilised and intelligent he really was, I would choose first not his trading activities, nor even his navigational and organisational skills, nor yet his artistry and craftsmanship except perhaps in shipbuilding, but his verbal skills. I frequently find it necessary to remind myself, in the words of a better scholar than myself, that in our reading of medieval literature we must always try to praise the right things for the right reasons. In accordance with that, I think we should praise skaldic poets for their highly developed verbal skill rather than for their perceptions of their world or for their inspiration or imagination. And in any case I believe that verbal skill is much more to their credit than anything else they might be said to have achieved. In the words of Bragi the Old (verse 300b): *hagsmiðr bragar—hvat er skáld nema þat?* (skilful craftsman of verse—what is a poet but that?)

REFERENCES

Carlyle, T. *On Heroes, Hero-Worship, and the Heroic in History.* London 1841. [Cited from the Centenary Edition, 1898]
Edda Snorra Sturlusonar. Ed. Finnur Jónsson. Copenhagen 1931.
Finnur Jónsson (ed.). *Den norsk-islandske Skjaldedigtning.* København 1912–15.
Foote, P. and Wilson, D. M. *The Viking Achievement.* London 1970.
Frank, R. *Old Norse Court Poetry: The Dróttkvætt Stanza.* Ithaca 1978.
ÍF = *Íslenzk fornrit* I ff. Reykjavík 1933– .
Kock, E. A. (ed.). *Den norsk-isländska skaldediktningen.* Lund 1946–9.
Kock, E. A. *Notationes norrœnae.* Lund 1923–46.
Kuhn, Hans. *Das Dróttkvætt.* Heidelberg 1983.
Macdonell, A. A. *A Vedic Reader for Students.* Madras 1917.
Magnús Ólafsson, *De poesi nostra discursus.* In Anthony Faulkes (ed.). *Two versions of Snorra Edda from the 17th Century* I, 408–15. Reykjavík 1979.
Marold, Edith. *Kenningkunst: Ein Beitrag zu einer Poetik der Skaldendichtung.* Berlin 1983.
Marold, Edith. 'Nýgerving und Nykrat'. *Twenty-eight papers presented to Hans Bekker-Nielsen on the occasion of his sixtieth birthday 28 April 1993.* Odense 1993, 283–302.
Mitchell, B. *An Invitation to Old English and Anglo-Saxon England.* Oxford 1995.
The Saga of Gisli. Trans. G. Johnston. London 1963.
Snorri Sturluson. *Edda: Háttatal.* Ed. Anthony Faulkes. Oxford 1991.
Spearing. A. C. *Readings in Medieval Poetry.* Cambridge 1989.
The Third and Fourth Grammatical Treatises. In Björn Magnússon Ólsen (ed.). *Den Tredje og Fjærde Grammatiske Afhandling i Snorres Edda.* København 1884.
Turville-Petre, E. O. G. *Scaldic Poetry.* Oxford 1976.
Wrenn, C. L. 'The Poetry of Caedmon'. *Proceedings of the British Academy* 1946, 277–95.